CW01431718

Original title:
Lanterned Echoes Around the Wizard Husk

Copyright © 2025 Swan Charm

Author: Kene Elistrand
ISBN HARDBACK: 978-1-80559-397-3
ISBN PAPERBACK: 978-1-80559-896-1

The Forgotten Glow of Ancient Tales

In shadows cast by time's embrace,
Echoes whisper of a distant place.
Where heroes roamed with hearts so bold,
And legends shimmered, rich with gold.

Through cracked maps and dusty scrolls,
The stories of the past still call.
With starlit skies and moonlit dreams,
They weave through life in silver streams.

A dragon's roar, a maiden's sigh,
In twilight's glow, their spirits fly.
Forgotten songs on gentle winds,
Through rustling leaves, the tale begins.

I wander through the ancient glade,
Where time's sweet pause no longer fades.
Once vibrant hearts that beat as one,
Now fade like dusk when day is done.

But through the mist of history,
A flicker burns in memory.
With every tale, the embers glow,
Reminding us of worlds we know.

Whispers of Glowing Orbs

In twilight's grace, the orbs unite,
They dance like stars, a gentle light.
With secrets shared in softest glow,
They whisper tales of long ago.

Beneath the sky, they flutter near,
A symphony for those who hear.
Moments caught in fleeting flight,
They spark the heart, ignite the night.

Shadows in the Enchanted Grove

In the grove where shadows play,
Mysteries swirl at end of day.
Ancient trees, with whispers deep,
Guard the dreams that nature keep.

Moonlight falls on velvet ground,
In silence, sacred stories found.
Echoes of lives, both lost and found,
In this haven, peace abounds.

Murmurs of the Forgotten Light

A flicker shines from depths of time,
In echoes soft, a distant chime.
With gentle hands, it reaches forth,
To stir the souls, and spark their worth.

In corners dark, where memories blend,
These whispers weave, and never end.
Each flicker tells a tale anew,
Of dreams deferred, and hopes that grew.

Flickering Dreams of the Night

In dreams that flicker like candle flames,
We chase the stories, call their names.
Each vision dances in the dark,
A spark of hope, a guiding mark.

When shadows beckon, and fears arise,
We grasp the light before our eyes.
In endless night, our spirits soar,
With flickering dreams, we seek for more.

Secret Gardens of Flickering Fireflies

In twilight's hush, they dance and gleam,
Whispers of magic in moonlight's beam.
Petals unfold, a soft, sweet sigh,
Where shadows play and dreamers lie.

Each flicker tells a tale untold,
Glowing secrets in the fold.
Nature's lanterns, bright and bold,
In secret gardens, life unfolds.

Beneath the mess of tangled vines,
Their silent glow, a sign that shines.
A world where wonder comes alive,
In the embrace of night, we thrive.

Butterflies flit from flower to flower,
In these gardens, time feels like power.
With every glow, a heart beats fast,
In fleeting moments that forever last.

Beneath the stars, beneath the trees,
We weave our dreams on gentle breeze.
In the flickering light, love is found,
In secret gardens, rich and sound.

Beneath the Glistening Abyss

In depths where shadows softly creep,
Where ancient currents swirl and sweep.
The ocean sings a haunting tune,
Underneath the silver moon.

Coral reefs in colors bright,
Flourish in the dark of night.
Mysteries wrapped in azure waves,
In the abyss, the soul it saves.

Whales' songs echo through the deep,
Cradling secrets in endless sleep.
With every pulse, the ocean breathes,
Wrapping dreams in silky sheaths.

Ghostly lights dance far below,
In twilight's arms, the wonders grow.
Creatures weave in a tranquil trance,
Inviting hearts to take a chance.

Beneath the glistening, dark expanse,
Life teems in a timeless dance.
In the ocean's embrace, we seek
The depths of love, both soft and sleek.

Illumination in the Foggy Halls

Through misty paths where whispers dwell,
Echoes of stories, they weave and tell.
Shadows linger, secrets flow,
In the fog, time moves slow.

Candles flicker, soft and warm,
In the chambers, a quiet charm.
Tales of old in silence speak,
Guiding souls who dare to seek.

Every corner holds a glance,
A flicker of fate, a silent chance.
Through foggy halls, we wander deep,
In search of dreams that we can keep.

Voices drift like ghosts of yore,
Binding us to ancient lore.
With every step, we find the glow,
Illuminating paths we sow.

In the heart of this swirling mist,
Every shadow has a tryst.
In foggy halls, with courage bright,
We embrace the tales of light.

Silken Threads of Stardust

In the cosmos, soft and bright,
Threads of stardust weave the night.
Each sparkle tells a tale so grand,
A universe, crafted by hand.

Galaxies swirl in a cosmic dance,
Unfolding dreams in a timeless trance.
With every shimmer, a wish takes flight,
In the embrace of the velvet night.

Celestial patterns, a tapestry spun,
Mapping journeys for everyone.
Beyond the limits of earthly care,
In stardust trails, we're free to dare.

Every heartbeat resonates true,
A melody old and forever new.
In this vastness, we find our role,
Stitched in the fabric, body, and soul.

Silken threads that bind us tight,
Connecting hearts in sheer delight.
Together we forge, in unity bright,
Under the watch of starlit night.

Gossamer Threads of Nighttime Sorcery

In shadows deep, the whispers weave,
A tapestry of dreams we believe.
Moonbeams dance on velvet skies,
As secrets stir in softest sighs.

Stars like jewels in the night's embrace,
Illuminating magic, a hidden trace.
The air is thick with ancient lore,
As midnight beckons, we explore.

Gossamer threads that shimmer bright,
Guide the way through the velvet night.
Each flicker a note in the cosmic song,
Where dreams and wishes all belong.

Winds carry tales of lost delight,
In each corner, shadows ignite.
Crafted spells in the cool night air,
Awakening wonders beyond compare.

As dawn approaches, the magic fades,
Yet in our hearts, the spark invades.
For every night, the sorcery's spun,
In gossamer threads, the world is one.

Twilight's Gleam in Enchanted Realms

Twilight whispers over hills so vast,
Painting skies with colors cast.
A soft embrace where dreams arise,
In enchanted realms beneath the skies.

Where echoes linger of ancient tales,
And the scent of magic gently hails.
Each shadow dances, spirits sing,
As twilight's glow begins to cling.

Mysterious paths in twilight's breath,
Lead us closer to the edge of myth.
With every step, the heart expands,
In timeless realms, the spirit stands.

Crickets sound their evening tune,
While fireflies light up the darkening moon.
In this magic hour of soft delight,
All hearts yearn to take flight.

As the day bows down to night's embrace,
We find ourselves in a sacred space.
For in twilight's gleam, we understand,
The threads of magic that weave this land.

Radiant Dreams in Sorcerous Swells

In ocean depths where wonders play,
Radiant dreams awaken the day.
Waves of magic roll and twine,
Whispers of fate in every sign.

Each surge is a spell, each crest a sigh,
Beneath the vast and endless sky.
In sorcerous swells, we dare to ride,
Where mysteries and wishes coincide.

Bubbles rise with hopes unspoken,
As ancient seals of silence broken.
The tides carry tales of heart's desire,
While sparks of light ignite the fire.

As moonlight bathes the sea in glow,
We twirl in currents, soft and slow.
For every dream is a treasure held,
In radiant swells where magic swelled.

And when we reach the shores of dawn,
With hearts ignited, we'll carry on.
For every wave that kissed the sand,
Left us with magic, hand in hand.

Twilight Lanterns, Whimsical Refrains

Twilight lanterns flicker bright,
Guiding dreams into the night.
Softly glowing, they lead the way,
In whimsical refrains, we sway.

Beneath the stars, our laughter flows,
As stories rise like gentle prose.
Each lantern brings a wish for flight,
In the symphony of the night.

Shadows dance where wishes gleam,
Cascading whispers, a secret dream.
With every flicker, a heart aglow,
In twilight's arms, we always know.

Moments stretch like ribbons spun,
In the magic where we are one.
Together, we weave the night's embrace,
In the tender glow, we find our place.

As dawn tiptoes on the crest of day,
The lanterns dim, yet memories stay.
For every refrain and every spark,
Lives forever in the twilight's dark.

The Soft Pulse of Hidden Magic

In shadows where whispers dwell,
Enchantment weaves its quiet spell.
Soft flickers dance in twilight glow,
A world of wonder starts to flow.

Secrets wrapped in velvet night,
Soft murmurs spark the heart's delight.
Threads of fate begin to twine,
In dreams where all the lost align.

Silent echoes fill the air,
Carrying tales of lost affair.
Each heartbeat sings a hidden truth,
A melody of endless youth.

In stillness, magic stirs awake,
Awakening the dreams we make.
With every pulse, a wish ignites,
Guiding souls to fated sights.

So let the soft pulse guide your way,
Through veils of night, toward the day.
For in the hidden, magic grows,
A soft pulse where divinity flows.

Glistening Memories in the Darkness

In the depth of shadowed sighs,
Glistening memories never die.
Like starlit drops on midnight dew,
They shimmer softly, wild and true.

Whispers of laughter linger near,
Carried by the winds we hear.
Each lingering note, a tale so sweet,
In darkness, where the heart might beat.

Fragments of joy from long ago,
In silence, they begin to show.
Each glimmer paints a story bright,
A canvas woven with pure light.

As time flows like a gentle stream,
Eternal echoes softly gleam.
In hidden corners of the mind,
Glistening memories entwined.

Embrace the warmth of what we know,
Let nostalgia's magic grow.
For in the darkness, hope will spark,
Glistening memories softly mark.

Twinkling Threads of Forgotten Sorcery

In a tapestry of night, we find,
Twinkling threads that softly bind.
They weave through dreams like whispered grace,
A touch of magic in time and space.

Lost spells dance in the twilight air,
Twisting through the heart's old lair.
Each glimmer holds a story spun,
Of sorcery where all begun.

In the depths of memory's fog,
Lies a flicker, a silent dialogue.
Forbidden tales in shadows hide,
Twinkling threads where secrets bide.

As we wander through forgotten lands,
We trace the patterns with our hands.
Each twinkling spark a wish fulfilled,
A magic longing to be thrilled.

Embrace the wonder, find the key,
Unlocking realms of mystery.
With twinkling threads, we're never lost,
For in this sorcery, we trust the cost.

Ripples of Enchantment Beneath Starlight

Beneath the stars, the waters flow,
Ripples of dreams begin to glow.
Each wave a whisper, soft and light,
Carried forth in the arms of night.

Enchantment swirls in moonlit beams,
Dancing lightly on silver streams.
Here magic sings on gentle tides,
In every ripple, hope abides.

Lost wishes float like petals down,
Where starlight weaves a velvet crown.
Each shimmer brings a tale to tell,
In the heart where fantasies dwell.

Look close at the path the water takes,
The magic flows, and the silence wakes.
Ripples of joy, a world unfurled,
In starlit whispers, a promise swirled.

As night embraces the sleeping earth,
Let enchantment fill your heart with mirth.
For beneath the starlight, dreams ignite,
Ripples of magic will guide your flight.

The Enchanted Tides of Radiant Mist

In the realm where moonlight sings,
Tides arrive with gentle rings,
Whispers dance on silver shores,
Carrying dreams forevermore.

Misty shrouds, a veil of dreams,
Guided by the starlit beams,
Nature's breath, a soft caress,
In this peace, our hearts confess.

Waves embrace the ancient stones,
Echoing with whispered tones,
Each ripple holds a story rare,
Of love and hope, beyond compare.

Shadows play in twilight's glow,
Painting tales of long ago,
As the night unfolds its art,
We find solace in the heart.

With every tide, life ebbs and flows,
In radiant mist, our spirit grows,
Expect the magic that awaits,
In enchanted tides, destiny waits.

Journey of the Glowing Spirits

Through the night, the spirits soar,
Guiding paths to distant shores,
With their light, we find our way,
In the whispers of the day.

Every flicker, a tale untold,
Of the brave and the bold,
They dance in the breeze, so free,
Leading us to destiny.

In the forest, where shadows play,
Glowing spirits guide our stay,
With each heartbeat, we align,
In the rhythm, pure and divine.

Stars above, our sacred map,
In the dark, they gently tap,
On the dreams that lie ahead,
Filling hearts with hope instead.

As the dawn begins to break,
We embrace the path we make,
With glowing spirits at our side,
In this journey, love's our guide.

Chasing Shadows in the Moon's Embrace

Underneath the silver glow,
Where the night's soft secrets flow,
Shadows dance with gentle grace,
In the moon's enchanted space.

Whispers fill the midnight air,
Tales of love and silent care,
Each shadow tells a story bright,
A dance of dreams in the night.

Chasing echoes, lost and found,
In the stillness, hearts unbound,
With every step, the journey flows,
Where the wild mystic wind blows.

Moonlight drapes the world in peace,
Resting souls find sweet release,
In the shadows, fears take flight,
Guided by the soft moonlight.

We embrace the night's soft call,
Learning how to rise and fall,
In the chase of shadows near,
We find strength and face our fear.

The Light of Wisdom Among the Lost

In the depths of wandering minds,
Wisdom waits and gently finds,
Those who seek through darkened haze,
A flicker of eternal blaze.

Among the lost, a spark ignites,
Guiding souls through endless nights,
With every step, the truth unfurls,
A light that glows within our worlds.

Questions rise like morning's dew,
Each answer brings a vision new,
In the quiet, the heart will learn,
To cherish every twist and turn.

Through trials faced, and shadows cast,
The wisdom found will ever last,
In the echoes of the past,
We harness strength, and fears outcast.

With light of wisdom shining bright,
We forge ahead, embrace the fight,
For among the lost, we shall see,
The paths that lead to our destiny.

Luminous Secrets of the Eldritch Empire

In ancient halls where shadows dwell,
Whispers echo, secrets tell.
Light cascades on stone and lore,
Unveiling paths of yore once more.

Mystics gather, their eyes ablaze,
With truths wrapped in a timeless haze.
The moonlight dances, softly bright,
Revealing wrongs, restoring right.

Lost tomes hidden beneath the dust,
Awakening dreams with fervent trust.
Eldritch hums in the midnight air,
Drawing all close to its silent glare.

With every flicker, shadows play,
While stars conspire in grand ballet.
An empire forged from forgotten grace,
In the luminous glow, we find our place.

Together we roam, free yet bound,
In the secrets of night, profound.
With every heartbeat, the cosmos sings,
Of luminous secrets and timeless rings.

Phantoms of Radiance in the Stillness

In the stillness, phantoms glide,
Carried softly on the tide.
In moonlit realms where silence reigns,
They whisper secrets, break the chains.

Radiance flickers like candle's glow,
Guiding lost hearts through the undertow.
Each breath a thread of mystic song,
Binding the night, where they belong.

Stars awaken with ancient eyes,
Dancing beneath the velvet skies.
Echoes of laughter, gentle and sweet,
In this stillness, souls we meet.

Awash in light, shadows convene,
On paths unknown, through spaces unseen.
Phantoms weave with ethereal grace,
In radiant glow, we find our place.

The night unfolds, a tapestry spun,
Illuminating journeys begun.
In silence we see, in stillness we find,
Phantoms of radiance intertwined.

Veils of Mystique in the Forest Depths

Veils of mystique cloak the trees,
Draped in whispers of the breeze.
Fern and shadow dance in rhyme,
Lost in the echoes of forgotten time.

Footfalls muted on the moss,
Guided by starlight's gentle gloss.
Within each glade, a secret sigh,
Stories of old that never die.

Light filters through, a golden beam,
Awakening memories from a dream.
In the depths where the wild things roam,
Nature's heart beats, calling us home.

Mysterious paths twist and twine,
Leading to realms where shadows align.
Every rustle, a call from fate,
In forest depths, we navigate.

With each step, the enchantment grows,
Of veils and whispers, the forest knows.
In the stillness, truths begin to seep,
In the mystique's embrace, our secrets keep.

The Flicker of Lost Spells

In twilight hours, where shadows blend,
Flickers of magic round corners bend.
Lost spells linger in the night's soft thrall,
Whispering dreams to those who call.

With open hearts and minds aglow,
We trace the paths that the ancients know.
Each whispered word, a gentle stir,
Awakening wonder that beckons us her.

In the flicker, lost moments rise,
Through veils of time, in silent skies.
Resurrected hopes dance in the air,
Like stars igniting a forgotten flare.

The past and present softly weave,
In the echoes of those who believe.
A tapestry of mysteries spun,
Beneath the moon, a journey begun.

Through the night, our spirits soar,
Finding magic on that distant shore.
In every flicker, hidden spells dwell,
A symphony of secrets, we weave so well.

Canvas of Echoes and Light

On a canvas stretched so wide,
Colors dance with joy and pride.
Brushstrokes whisper tales so bright,
Echoing warmth in soft sunlight.

Each hue a memory held dear,
Past and future draw so near.
In the blend of dark and light,
Life's essence shines with pure delight.

Fragments of dreams in tides of gold,
Stories of the brave and bold.
Splashing colors, faint and bright,
Creating magic in pure sight.

A frame of moments lost in time,
Rhythms pulse, a whispered chime.
Artistry with every heart,
In this world, we all take part.

Borders blur, and boundaries fade,
In this masterpiece we've made.
Canvas holds the silent fight,
Echoes crafted in sheer light.

Ethereal Whispers in the Gloom

In the stillness of the night,
Whispers float, a ghostly flight.
Ethereal dreams hang in the air,
Soft and fragile, oh so rare.

Shadows dance beneath the moon,
Carrying secrets like a tune.
Each sigh a story, lost in time,
Echoes linger, nearly rhyme.

Voices murmur from the deep,
Calling forth the souls that weep.
In the gloom where spirits roam,
They return to seek a home.

Flickering lights, a fleeting glance,
Embers whisper in their dance.
Life and death, a tender thread,
Woven paths where hearts have tread.

In the quiet, truth unfurls,
Every echo swirls and whirls.
Ethereal whispers, soft and low,
Guiding us where we must go.

Veils of Light and Shadow Play

In the twilight's gentle blush,
Veils of light begin to rush.
Shadows stretch and intertwine,
Creating patterns, so divine.

Light spills gold on fields of gray,
Painting dreams where shadows sway.
In the dance of dusk and dawn,
Worlds awaken, fears are gone.

Every flicker, every hue,
Tells a tale, both old and new.
Veils that spin in vibrant ways,
Casting spells of warm dismay.

Whispers weave between the trees,
Rustling gently with the breeze.
Nature's canvas, wild and free,
Light and shadow blend in harmony.

In this play, we find our place,
Entwined in time, a soft embrace.
Veils of light and shadow play,
A beautiful end to the day.

Sparkling Legends in the Twilight

Beneath the arch of twilight skies,
Legends sparkle, never die.
Stories twinkle, bright as stars,
Whispered softly, near and far.

Moonlit paths of shimmering gold,
Time-touched tales of brave and bold.
Every twinkle holds a dream,
An endless echo, flowing stream.

Heroes rise in whispered light,
Fighting shadows, claiming flight.
In the twilight, fears dissolve,
Mysteries around us resolve.

Glimmers dance on waters bright,
Casting shadows into night.
Every heart beats with a flame,
In sparkling legends, we find fame.

As stardust falls, our spirits soar,
In twilight's glow, we seek for more.
Legends woven in time's embrace,
Sparkling truths we dare to chase.

Dreams Illuminated by Myth

In twilight's grasp, the stories wake,
With whispers soft, the ancients speak.
A tapestry of stars above,
In shadows cast, we find our love.

Beneath the veil of night they dance,
Timeless tales in a fleeting glance.
Every heartbeat echoes fate,
In dreams, we learn to navigate.

Wonders bloom in realms unseen,
Where magic flows and minds convene.
With every myth, we come alive,
In dreams, the spirit starts to thrive.

A phoenix rises, radiant, bold,
In every dream, a story told.
Through whispered winds, our hopes take flight,
In mythic lands, we embrace the night.

So chase the dreams, let spirits soar,
In every myth, there's so much more.
With open hearts, let's weave our tale,
In dreams illuminated, we shall prevail.

Shattered Light in the Wilderness

Beneath the towering trees so grand,
Shadows flicker across the land.
Echoes of light, a fragile thread,
In the wilderness, the lost are led.

Through brambles thick and paths unclear,
The heart beats loud, drowning in fear.
Where silence reigns, the spirits sigh,
In shatters of light, we learn to fly.

Whispers of wind tell stories untold,
Of dreams once bright, now dulled and cold.
Yet in the dark, we glimpse the spark,
A flicker of hope in the dewy park.

With every step, we seek the sun,
In shattered light, we become one.
In every shadow, there's a flame,
A reminder that we're all the same.

So breathe the wild, let it in,
In shattered light, we find our kin.
Together we rise, together we roam,
In the wilderness, we find our home.

Mystical Sighs in the Moonlit Wood

In the heart of woods, where shadows play,
The moon bestows its silver ray.
Whispers echo through ancient trees,
Mystical sighs ride on the breeze.

With every step, the world fades away,
The forest hums a gentle sway.
Each leaf drops secrets, softly drawn,
In moonlit glow, the magic's born.

The nightingale sings a haunting song,
In the wood, we all belong.
With every note, the spirits glide,
Through mystical sighs, we turn the tide.

The starlit paths weave tales divine,
In moonlit wood, we drink the wine.
A harmony of peace unfolds,
In every silence, a story told.

So linger softly, breathe it in,
In the moonlit wood, we begin.
With every sigh, our dreams align,
In mystical realms, our hearts entwine.

Symbols of the Wandering Fire

Around the flames, our shadows leap,
In dancing lights, secrets we keep.
Every spark, a tale ignites,
Symbols weave through the starry nights.

Embers whisper of journeys past,
Through wandering fires, our dreams are cast.
With every glow, we chase the sun,
In laughter shared, our hearts are one.

Flickering shadows play on the ground,
In circles drawn, our souls are found.
Through crackling wood, our voices rise,
In symbols of fire, we touch the skies.

The night unveils its vibrant hue,
With every warmth, we discover truth.
In every flame, a vision clear,
In wandering fire, we conquer fear.

So gather near, let stories flow,
In symbols bright, let love bestow.
Through flames that dance, we learn to soar,
In wandering fire, we are evermore.

Ethereal Sounds in the Forest's Heart

Whispers glide through ancient trees,
Melodies of leaves in gentle breeze.
Echoes dance beneath the moon,
Nature sings a timeless tune.

Crickets chirp, a soft refrain,
Flowing streams, the sweet domain.
Rustling ferns, a hushed delight,
Cradling dreams of purest night.

Owls call out, their wisdom shared,
In the dark, the night is bared.
Magic blooms in every sound,
Harmony in silence found.

Footfalls light on mossy ground,
Every step a sacred sound.
In the heart where spirits roam,
The forest whispers, "You are home."

Stars above in quiet gleam,
Nature's pulse, a vibrant dream.
Ethereal sounds ignite the soul,
In the woods, we feel whole.

Dappled Light on Mystic Waves

Sunbeams dance on waters blue,
Kissing ripples, fresh and new.
Whispers of the ocean's grace,
In the depths, time leaves no trace.

Seagulls soar on gentle winds,
Where the water's song begins.
Dappled light in playful glance,
Nature invites us to the dance.

Shells and shadows intertwine,
In this realm where dreams align.
Waves embrace the golden shore,
Each retreat opens up a door.

The tide reveals what lies beneath,
Silent secrets, nature's wreath.
With each pulse, the heart will find,
Mystic waves that soothe the mind.

In the silence, echoes stay,
Guiding souls along the way.
Dappled light, a soft caress,
In this world, we are blessed.

The Alchemy of Shadows and Light

In twilight's grasp, the shadows blend,
Soft whispers of the day's end.
Light cascades on edges near,
Transforming night, dispelling fear.

Figures dance in flickered glow,
Stories told in ebb and flow.
Mysteries wrapped in twilight's veil,
Shadows weave the nightingale.

Golden beams through leaves shall seep,
Awakening the world from sleep.
Secrets linger, softly bright,
In the alchemy of night.

As stars awaken, dreams resume,
In the dark, new worlds bloom.
Shadows shift with grace and charm,
Carrying both calm and alarm.

In every hue, the heart ignites,
Crafting tales of days and nights.
The alchemy of dusk unfolds,
With shadows deep, a life retold.

Reverberations of Nightfall's Charm

Moonlight spills across the land,
Casting dreams with gentle hand.
A symphony of stars ignite,
Whispering tales of endless night.

Crickets hum their softest song,
In the dark where whispers throng.
Every rustle holds a secret,
Nightfall's charm, the soul shall greet.

Breezes carry scents of dawn,
As the shadows begin to yawn.
Glimmers play along the stream,
Chasing echoes of a dream.

Candles flicker, shadows swell,
In this hush, we know it well.
Reverberations through the trees,
Nightfall's magic on the breeze.

With every breath, the world seems clear,
In the dark, we shed our fear.
Embracing night with open heart,
In reverberations, we won't part.

The Lure of Radiant Memories

In the dawn's soft light, they gleam,
Shadows dancing, a fleeting dream.
Whispers echo, like a song,
In my heart, where they belong.

Laughter spills from a distant space,
Moments held in time's embrace.
Faded pictures, vivid hues,
Tales of joy we dare not lose.

Through the years, they call my name,
A flicker of love, a gentle flame.
Golden threads that weave the past,
In the tapestry, they hold fast.

As twilight wraps the world in peace,
The glow of memory will not cease.
Each recollection, a guiding star,
Illumined paths, no matter how far.

In quiet moments, they unfold,
Stories wrapped in threads of gold.
The lure of memories, shining bright,
Guiding us through the velvet night.

Reflections of the Unearthly

In the stillness of a hidden grove,
Whispers of ancient secrets rove.
Stars adorn the midnight sky,
Under their watchful gaze, we lie.

Mirrored pools of silver light,
Capture dreams that take to flight.
Echoes of an ethereal song,
In this realm, we all belong.

Veils of mist weave 'round our souls,
Guided by thoughts that time extols.
In the depths, where shadows play,
Reflections dance and drift away.

The air is thick with tales untold,
Of mystical wonders, brave and bold.
Through the night, we seek to find,
The hidden truths that bind mankind.

As dawn approaches, light will break,
Revealing paths that dreams will make.
In the dawn, the spirits flee,
Leaving their whispers, wild and free.

The Soft Whisper of Glowing Beacons

Across the night, they pierce the dark,
Glowing beacons, each a spark.
Softly calling from the shore,
Guiding souls forevermore.

Candles flicker in windows wide,
Where hopes and dreams do safely hide.
Their warm embrace, a gentle guide,
As we wander, side by side.

Lanterns sway in twilight's breath,
Illuminating paths to rest.
With every flicker, tales arise,
Of love that never says goodbye.

The soft whisper of their glow,
Leads us where our hearts can flow.
In this dance of light and shade,
The warmth of memories never fades.

Through the night, we find our way,
Haloed in the silver sway.
With glowing beacons by our side,
Together, we will always glide.

Fantasies in the Shimmering Breeze

On a shore where dreams collide,
Waves of wonder, hearts open wide.
The shimmering breeze carries tales,
Of fantasy where love prevails.

Dancing reflections on the sea,
Questions floating, wild and free.
Whispers of wishes in the air,
Entwined with hopes beyond compare.

Through the gardens where shadows play,
Colors burst at break of day.
Each petal holds a secret song,
In this realm, we all belong.

As twilight deepens, dreams take flight,
Illuminated by the night.
With every breath, the magic stirs,
In the silence, our spirit purrs.

Fantasies weave through the trees,
Guided by that shimmering breeze.
Together we soar, hearts unconfined,
In the world where dreams entwined.

Magic's Pulse Beneath Wistful Boughs

In the whispering woods where shadows play,
Ancient spirits dance through the twilight sway.
Each rustle and sigh, a secret untold,
As dreams take flight, in the heart they unfold.

Beneath the boughs, where the faeries dwell,
The moon weaves a spell, a luminous swell.
With glimmers of hope in the soft evening light,
The night blooms alive, a serene, gentle sight.

Roots intertwine in a timeless embrace,
The pulse of the earth beats at a slow pace.
With echoes of laughter, the leaves softly hum,
In the magic of night, all worries become numb.

Candles ignite in the heart of the glade,
While whispers of wishes like silk thread are laid.
With each flickering flame, a story is spun,
As stars wink above, their watch just begun.

In the hush of the twilight, where moments reside,
The night gently cradles the dreams that abide.
With every soft sigh, a new chapter unfurls,
In the cradle of night, we explore other worlds.

Ethereal Light in the Arcane Night

Under a tapestry of darkened skies,
Magic descends where the dreamer lies.
With shimmering threads of an ancient delight,
Ethereal glow leads the lost through the night.

In the stillness of time, the secrets convene,
Revealing their truths, serene and unseen.
Winds carry whispers, a haunting refrain,
Stirring the heart with a thrill of the arcane.

The moonlight cascades, a river of grace,
Illuminating the dreams time cannot erase.
With every soft shadow that weaves through the air,
The enchantment of night fills the soul with care.

In corners forgotten, the magic awakes,
As stardust embraces the dreams that it makes.
With pathways of light, the unseen shall guide,
Through realms of the night, let the heart be your stride.

Thus dance with the magic, in silence it glows,
The arcane reveals what the universe knows.
Beneath the heavens deep, let the spirit take flight,
Kindled by the ethereal light of the night.

Secrets of Fables Adrift in Luminance

In the glimmer of dawn, where stories reside,
Secrets emerge as the shadows divide.
With each whispered fable, a tale takes its form,
Drifting like clouds in a sun-kissed warm storm.

The pages of time, in a flutter, unfold,
Revealing their wisdom, like treasures of gold.
In whispering breezes, the echoes once spun,
Dance like the leaves in the warmth of the sun.

Within the embrace of the luminous skies,
Legends awaken, where the heart never lies.
Each flicker of light holds a moment divine,
As dreams weave together, like threads in design.

From valleys of lore to the heights of delight,
Adventures unfold in a tapestry bright.
As paths intertwine in the stories we share,
Luminance carries us to places so rare.

In the secret of fables, let wonder ignite,
For every soft whisper holds magic in sight.
With hearts ever open, we'll journey anew,
In the embrace of each tale, let the spirit renew.

The Mystique of Celestial Echoes

In the vast expanse where starlight bends,
Celestial echoes weave the night's ends.
Each twinkle a whisper, calling us near,
Guiding lost souls through the cosmic frontier.

Beyond the horizon, where dreams intertwine,
Lies a world of wonders, both yours and divine.
With shimmering trails, the galaxies hum,
In the quiet of space, where sailors become.

Through the veil of the night, the mysteries play,
With planets and comets in an elegant sway.
In the dance of existence, the heart finds its pace,
As shadows of stardust brush against timeless space.

In echoes of laughter, the cosmos will sing,
In the silence of stars, new beginnings take wing.
With each whispered secret, let spirits ignite,
For the mysteries linger in the depth of the night.

So dream with the heavens, let wonder arise,
In the mystique of night, find the light in the skies.
As celestial echoes cradle us tight,
We're woven together by the fabric of night.

The Enigma of Shimmering Fog

In valleys deep, where silence clings,
Shimmering fog in twilight sings.
Whispers fade, as shadows blend,
Secrets held, they never end.

A canvas gray, with hints of light,
Mysteries born in fading night.
Footsteps echo on a winding trail,
Guided by dreams where senses fail.

Veils of gray kiss the trees,
Dancing soft in evening breeze.
Lost in thought, where visions play,
The enigma fades with break of day.

A fleeting glimpse, a heartbeat caught,
In this fog, what battles fought?
As dawn emerges, all is clear,
Yet still, the questions linger near.

Through layers thick, the world unfolds,
In shimmering mists, the heart beholds.
Each breath a new, uncharted course,
In every fog, a hidden force.

Ethereal Lights Beyond the Mist

In realms where shadows softly play,
Ethereal lights beckon, sway.
Glowing trails through twilight air,
Calling seekers unaware.

Veils parted in the silent night,
Flickering softly, a wondrous sight.
Colors merging, a gentle flow,
Beyond the mist, where dreamers go.

A world untouched by time's embrace,
Filling hearts with quiet grace.
Footsteps follow, hesitant glow,
Chasing wonders hidden low.

Whispers echo in the air,
Memories linger, tales to share.
In the glow, all fears dissolve,
As mysteries deep gradually evolve.

With every step, the light reveals,
Lost desires, the heart appeals.
In this land of soft delight,
Ethereal dreams take flight tonight.

Radiant Reflections in Ancient Woods

Amidst the trees, where time stands still,
Radiant reflections bend and thrill.
Golden beams through branches weave,
Ancient woods, a tale to conceive.

Leaves rustle in the gentle breeze,
Whispers of past, carried with ease.
Mossy carpets, shadows cast,
Faded stories of ages past.

Silvery streams reflect the sky,
Mirroring dreams that float nearby.
Each bubble bursts with tales of yore,
Echoing secrets from forest floor.

In stillness, moments intertwine,
Radiance glows, like aged wine.
Every glance, a spark ignites,
In the heart of woods, our soul takes flight.

Underneath the ancient boughs,
Nature's rhythm softly bows.
Reflecting light, inviting grace,
In these woods, we find our place.

The Dance of Silhouettes Under Moonlight

Under moonlight's silver glow,
Silhouettes sway, a gentle flow.
Figures dance in twilight's trance,
Lost in shadows, they twirl and prance.

Whispers carried on cool night air,
A melody found, beyond compare.
Every movement, an age-old song,
In this place where dreams belong.

Branches scratch against the night,
Creating patterns, pure delight.
Echoes lingering in the dark,
Sparking life, igniting a spark.

Beneath the watchful, gazing moon,
Silhouettes dance to nature's tune.
Lost in rhythm, hearts confess,
In every twirl, the night's caress.

A fleeting glance, a moment shared,
In shadowed forms, we are unpared.
Together we weave through the night,
In the dance of silhouettes, pure light.

Nightfall's Embrace on the Mystic Trail

In twilight's glow, shadows dance slow,
Whispers of night, where secrets flow.
Stars flicker bright, in celestial hues,
Guiding the lost, with ancient clues.

Moonlight bathes the path in silver lace,
Mystic trails weave through time and space.
Each rustling leaf sings a tale untold,
Of wanderers brave, and spirits bold.

The air is thick with a sweet, strange scent,
Of dreams unspooled, where moments are spent.
Through winding woods, the echoes draw near,
In nightfall's embrace, there's nothing to fear.

A lantern glows with the hope of dawn,
Chasing the shadows that linger on.
Every heartbeat thrums with a quiet grace,
In the arms of night, we find our place.

Echoing Footsteps in the Realm of Dreams

In realms where the lost and found collide,
Footsteps echo, where wishes reside.
A tapestry woven in midnight's thread,
Guides the heart where the restless tread.

Gentle whispers on a velvet breeze,
Calling the dreamers with playful tease.
With every step, a forgotten song,
In the realm of dreams, we all belong.

Chasing shadows through the misty haze,
Each turn reveals a labyrinth's maze.
The laughter of stars, a sweet serenade,
As time slips away, unafraid.

Awash in colors of twilight's charm,
Finding solace in the night's arm.
Every heartbeat marks the pulse of time,
In this ethereal realm, we climb.

Shimmering Paths of Aether

Across the skies, where stardust gleams,
Shimmering paths weave through our dreams.
A dance of light in the cosmic sea,
Inviting all souls to wander free.

Each step taken sparks a vibrant hue,
A tapestry spun with wishes anew.
Galaxies swirl as thoughts intertwine,
In the heart of aether, divine design.

Floating whispers rush through the air,
Carrying echoes of love and care.
Through shimmering realms where the heart retreats,
Eternal journeys with bittersweet beats.

As dawn approaches with a tender touch,
The paths of aether softly clutch.
Holding close the tales of the night,
In shimmering paths, we find our light.

Whims of the Ethereal Spirits

In the twilight's hush, the spirits play,
Whims of the ethereal lead the way.
They flutter like shadows, light as a sigh,
In the moon's embrace, they soar and fly.

Through enchanted groves, they laugh and spin,
Inviting lost hearts to dance within.
Their laughter, a breeze that tickles the trees,
Carrying dreams on a sweet, soft breeze.

Each flicker of light a secret shared,
In the whispers of night, love is declared.
With every heartbeat, the magic flows,
In the realm of spirits, our essence grows.

A tapestry woven of stars and dreams,
In the dance of the night, everything gleams.
As dawn approaches, they fade from view,
Whims of the ethereal, forever true.

Resonating Light Among the Ancient Trees

Whispers of the wind do roam,
Beneath the boughs, a secret home.
Sunlight dances through the leaves,
Nature's magic, one believes.

Shadows play upon the ground,
Footfalls soft, no harsh sound found.
Every sigh of leaf and bark,
Echoes secrets, deep and dark.

In the twilight, colors blend,
Crimson, gold, it seems to send.
A chorus fills the quiet air,
Of ancient tales, beyond compare.

Branches twist in gentle grace,
Framing sky, a sacred space.
Light reveals a hidden path,
Where dreams linger, free from wrath.

A symphony of heartbeats hum,
In nature's arms, we all become.
Resonating, lost and found,
Among the trees, our souls unbound.

Luminescent Serenades in the Mist

Through the fog, a soft glow gleams,
Nighttime whispers, carrying dreams.
With each step, the world transforms,
Underneath the moonlit forms.

Silhouettes of branches sway,
As the shadows dance and play.
Gentle breezes hum a tune,
Woven hopes beneath the moon.

Pale reflections shimmer bright,
Splashing colors in the night.
Misty trails of silver lace,
Lead us softly, trace by trace.

Every breath, a fleeting note,
On the wind, a haunting quote.
Serenades of calm descend,
In the twilight, time does bend.

Lost in wonder, hearts take flight,
Beneath the stars, a sacred sight.
Luminescent dreams ignite,
In the silence, pure delight.

Heartbeats of Magic in the Shadows

In the corners where night dwells,
Echoes shimmer, casting spells.
Flickers of a hidden spark,
Dance alive within the dark.

Every heartbeat whispers low,
Stirring secrets, ebb and flow.
Magic lingers in the air,
As if dreams are woven there.

Softly, twilight weaves its thread,
Through the thoughts we've left unsaid.
Shadows murmur, beckon near,
Inviting whispers we can hear.

Underneath the canopy,
Mysteries entwined, set free.
Time slows down, a gentle tune,
Guided softly by the moon.

Amongst the echoes and the night,
We find solace, pure delight.
Heartbeats pulse, a rhythm true,
Magic thrives in me and you.

The Allure of the Wandering Lights

Flickering softly, they appear,
Guiding hearts, chasing fear.
Wandering lights, a playful tease,
In the night, they drift with ease.

Through the dark, they spin and swirl,
Each a promise, a mystic whirl.
Entranced, we follow their embrace,
A journey through this sacred space.

With each flicker, hopes ignite,
Painting dreams across the night.
Whispers call from all around,
In their magic, we are found.

Dancing flames, forever bright,
Lighting paths through endless night.
In this moment, we belong,
As the stars hum their soft song.

The allure of lights that roam,
Draws us closer to the unknown.
In their glow, we find our way,
And chase the night till break of day.

Twilight's Gentle Embrace of Its Children

The sun dips low, a golden hue,
Soft shadows stretch where flowers grew.
Whispers of night begin to dance,
In twilight's hold, we take a chance.

Cool breezes weave through branches high,
Crickets chirp as the day says goodbye.
The stars awaken, one by one,
Embracing the night, the day is done.

A palette painted bold and bright,
Colors of dusk, a stunning sight.
The moon ascends, its gentle glow,
Guides the lost hearts, soft and slow.

Children laugh under sky's embrace,
Chasing dreams in a quiet space.
Each breath a prayer, each sigh a song,
In twilight, we find where we belong.

Magic lingers in the fading light,
Promises whispered to the night.
With every star, a wish is made,
In twilight's arms, our fears will fade.

Glimmers of Enigma in Flickering Silhouettes

In shadows cast by moon's soft glow,
Mysterious forms begin to flow.
Each rustling leaf, a secret shared,
Echoes of voices, faintly bared.

Dim light reveals tales of the past,
Flickering hopes that hold us fast.
Glimmers of thoughts, like stars alight,
Illuminate paths in the heart of night.

Whispers of pain and songs of joy,
Entwined together, no time to destroy.
Silhouettes dance in the cool midnight,
A ballet woven from dark and light.

Lurking doubts fade into the mist,
Held by the dreams we can't resist.
Every heartbeat, a rhythm true,
In flickering lights, our spirits renew.

As dawn approaches, they disappear,
The enigma whispers, stay near, stay near.
In the silence, secrets remain,
Glimmers of hope softly sustain.

Celestial Echoes Beneath the Ancient Sky

Under the vast and twinkling dome,
Ancient wisdom finds a home.
Echoes of starlight gently fall,
Whispering tales of the ages' call.

Galaxies swirl, dance in the night,
A cosmic ballet, a stunning sight.
Each heartbeat resonates through the air,
Celestial melodies, pure and rare.

Beneath this sky, we ponder deep,
Awake to wonder, wake from sleep.
The universe sings in every breath,
Lives entwined, for love, or death.

Wonders of time flow like a stream,
In dreams we seek, in dreams we beam.
Cosmologies painted with vibrant strokes,
Each star a muse, each night a cloak.

Here in the silence, we all conspire,
A hunger for truth, a heart's desire.
As echoes fade, our spirits soar,
Touched by the night, forever more.

The Whispering Glow of Lost Flutes

In the distance, a melody weeps,
Echoes of flutes where silence sleeps.
Notes drift softly through twilight's veil,
Carried by whispers, a haunting trail.

Once played by hands that long have passed,
Their music lingers, forever cast.
A story woven in every tune,
Under the gaze of the watchful moon.

The air shimmers with fleeting grace,
Filling the night, a sweet embrace.
Fingers on flutes, lost to time,
Resonate softly, like a chime.

Memories dance, elusive and bright,
In every note, a glimpse of light.
Unseen artists, ghosts of the past,
Crafting melodies that ever last.

So let the flutes breathe once again,
Reviving our souls, our hearts' own den.
In the night's cradle, sweet music sways,
A whisper of dreams in the moon's soft gaze.

Enigmatic Lullabies from the Astral Realm

In the silence of glimmering dreams,
Songs of the cosmos softly stream.
Lullabies weave through the night,
Stars whisper secrets of forgotten light.

Clouds of silver drift and wane,
Carrying echoes of joy and pain.
Each note a story gently spun,
Beyond the reach of anyone.

Galaxies hum in a tender embrace,
Tracing the paths of time and space.
Celestial rhythms hold us tight,
Guiding us through the endless night.

Softly, the aura begins to fade,
As the universe serenely played.
Bathed in dreams, we find our peace,
In the astral realm, sorrows cease.

Awake, awake to the dawning light,
Let the melodies dance in flight.
For every end holds a new refrain,
In the lullabies of love, there is no pain.

Glimmers of Sorrows Wrapped in Magic

Beneath the veil of a twilight shroud,
Glimmers of sorrows softly loud.
Wrapped in the magic of shadows deep,
Whispers of worlds where lost dreams sleep.

Each glimmer holds a tale of woe,
Stories buried where wild winds blow.
Yet in their glow, hope arises,
Sparkling like stars in hidden disguises.

Silken threads of fate entwine,
Drawing hearts to the edges of time.
For every tear, a spell is cast,
Binding the future to the past.

In the moonlight, heartaches gleam,
Weaving a tapestry, a delicate dream.
With every sigh, magic unfolds,
Glimmers of courage, cherished and bold.

So take these fires, burn them bright,
Transforming darkness into light.
For sorrow's song, though bittersweet,
Wraps us in magic, a love complete.

Whispers from the Woven Wild

In the heart of the woods, secrets stir,
Whispers of nature, a tender purr.
Leaves rustle softly in the breeze,
Carrying stories through the trees.

Creatures of magic glide and play,
Dancing in circles 'til break of day.
Their laughter echoes, bright and clear,
Binding the wild with dreams and cheer.

Roots entwined in the earth below,
Cradle the wisdom of all we know.
Each shadow and light, a tale unspun,
Whispers entwined, the wild has begun.

Celestial bodies watch from above,
Showering the world with endless love.
In twilight hours, where spirits roam,
The woven wild calls us home.

So let us wander through emerald glades,
Where every path and whisper parades.
In the woven wild, we shall find,
The magic that binds all hearts and minds.

Twilight's Play in Ocean of Stars

As twilight descends, the stars ignite,
Painting the sky with shimmering light.
An ocean of dreams before our gaze,
Whispers of time in a cosmic haze.

The waves of night serenely swell,
Carrying secrets they'll never tell.
Each ripple a note in nature's song,
In the ocean of stars where we belong.

Glimmers of hope ride the lunar tides,
Where magic and wonder gently collide.
Over horizons, the shadows play,
In the embrace of night, dreams find their way.

As constellations weave their tales,
Guiding the weary where silence prevails.
In twilight's glow, our spirits soar,
In an ocean of stars, forevermore.

So gaze at the heavens, let worries cease,
In this cosmic dance, we find our peace.
For twilight's play, like a lover's sigh,
Lifts our souls to the endless sky.

Phosphorescent Whispers of the Arcane

Soft glimmers pulse with secrets untold,
Faint echoes weave through the night's cold.
Mysteries cradle each luminous breath,
In shadows where whispers dance with death.

Stars awaken in a twilight embrace,
Unraveling stories etched in space.
Fabled dreams drift on gossamer wings,
Binding what magic in foresight brings.

Eldritch charms beckon the brave of heart,
In twilight lands where the ancients part.
With every flicker, new worlds ignite,
Illusions woven in the fabric of night.

Visions twine into the midnight air,
Enshrouded in wonders beyond compare.
In phosphorescent hues, we find our way,
As the arcane whispers beckon and sway.

Shadows Dancing in Mirthful Gleam

In the moonlight's playful caress,
Shadows twirl with joyous finesse.
Laughter echoes through the deep wood,
Where daylight dared not to intrude.

Glimmers of starlight tie their fate,
As creatures of night begin to skate.
In the hush of dusk, they gather near,
For revelry whispered, drawn so clear.

Joyful spirits spin in delight,
Casting their spells in the soft twilight.
Each flicker of whimsy, a gentle tease,
Swaying softly in the cool evening breeze.

Mirthful reflection on twinkling streams,
Where shadows dance in twilit dreams.
In this playful charade, time stands still,
And echoes of laughter linger at will.

In their carefree pirouettes and plays,
Shadows muster the magic of days.
Their joyful spirit in every beam,
Forever weaving in the twilight's dream.

Enchanted Flickers Beneath Twilight Canopies

Beneath the boughs of twilight trees,
Whispers float on a gentle breeze.
Flickers of wonder dance through the grove,
In the silence where magic roves.

Enchantments twine in the gloaming light,
Painting the world in hues so bright.
With each step taken beneath the stars,
Dreams unfold as if chasing cars.

A symphony hums in the vibrant dusk,
Filled with scents of earth and musk.
Leaves shimmer, kissed by the evening's glow,
In enchanted realms where wishes flow.

The moon hangs low with a knowing glance,
Inviting secrets to take a chance.
Flickers ignite the night's deep reign,
As twilight weaves its tender chain.

In harmony, nature breathes and sighs,
As dreams are born and never die.
Beneath these canopies, life's a play,
In every enchanted flicker, we sway.

Resounding Tales from the Elderwood Enclave

In the heart of the woods where legends dwell,
Ancient spirits weave their spell.
Each twist of bark, a memory sings,
Echoes of time among living things.

Resounding whispers on the forest floor,
Tales of the past forevermore.
Gnarled branches twist in heartfelt guise,
Holding secrets beneath the skies.

As night drapes its cloak, shadows arise,
Transporting us back to where wisdom lies.
With murmurs that flutter in soft twilight,
The elderwood shares its stories bright.

In the laughter of leaves, we find our kin,
A promise of what waits deep within.
Through moonlit paths, we wander and roam,
Finding our tales, our heartbeats' home.

Within each echo, adventures wait,
As time weaves together our fateful state.
In the elderwood's embrace, we shall find,
The resounding tales that bind our kind.

Elysian Reverberations from Timeless Ruins

In the hush where whispers dwell,
Forgotten tales begin to swell.
Echoes dance in ancient air,
Time's embrace, a gentle flair.

Crumbled stones with stories sung,
In shadows deep, the past is young.
Nature weaves its soft refrain,
Beneath the moonlight's gentle reign.

Violet blooms take root in grace,
Memories linger in their space.
Each petal tells a tale unspun,
Of all the battles lost and won.

Golden rays in twilight's arms,
Feel the pull of ancient charms.
Hearts entwined with history,
In ruins shrouded, wild and free.

So walk with me through ages lost,
Embrace the echoes, count the cost.
Elysian fields await our gaze,
In reverberations, lost in haze.

Glimmers of the Arcane Night

Stars unfold their mystic light,
Weaving dreams in endless night.
Whispers of the ancient lore,
Draw us closer to the shore.

Beneath the veil of twilight's hue,
Secrets linger, fresh and new.
Moonlit paths of silver bright,
Guide our hearts in shared delight.

Winds of magic softly call,
Every shadow, every thrall.
Veiled in whispers, time and space,
In this dance, we find our place.

Crystals glisten, reflect the sky,
In the hush, we learn to fly.
Glimmers spark with every sigh,
In this moment, we defy.

So breathe the night, embrace the dreams,
Let your soul weave through the seams.
In the arcane's tender night,
We find solace, pure and bright.

Celestial Murmurs in the Wind

Whispers float on whispered sighs,
Carried forth beneath the skies.
Stars entwine in cosmic grace,
Winds of fate, a soft embrace.

Laughter lingers, eternal sound,
In the breeze, our hopes are found.
Echoes ripple, tender phrases,
Dancing lightly through the mazes.

Timeless tales in twilight chime,
Secrets spoken, bridge of rhyme.
Through the night, our spirits soar,
Celestial realms, forevermore.

Gaze above, where dreams reside,
In the vastness, we confide.
Murmurs gentle, sweet and kind,
In the wind, our souls aligned.

So listen close, let your heart hear,
Every note both far and near.
In this song, we find our kin,
Celestial murmurs in the wind.

Where Shadows Play with Light

In dusk's embrace, the shadows sigh,
A ballet where the soft light lies.
Figures dance in twilight's air,
Painted scenes, a quiet prayer.

Flickers tease the edges near,
Hints of laughter, whispers clear.
Echoes pulse, a rhythmic fight,
Where shadows waltz with fleeting light.

Shapes converge and then disperse,
In this dream, we converse.
Illusions weave and drift afar,
Clothed in night, the fleeting star.

Crimson hues of fading day,
Casts their warmth, then slips away.
Yet in this dance, we find delight,
As shadows play with gentle light.

And when the darkness steals in close,
Remember well what hearts engross.
For in the night, so wild and bright,
We find our truth where shadows light.

Celestial Glimmers Amidst Bewitching Silence

In the stillness of night's embrace,
Stars whisper tales, a secret place.
The moonlight dances on silver streams,
Heartbeats echo with dreams and gleams.

Silhouettes of trees sway soft and low,
As shadows paint the world below.
Each flicker tells of wonders bright,
A cosmic show in the tranquil light.

Beneath the vast and endless sky,
Hope springs forth as the nightbirds fly.
In silence wrapped, the beauty grows,
A harmony that nature knows.

Whispers linger in fragrant air,
Echoes of magic, beyond compare.
With every sigh of the gentle breeze,
The night unveils its mysteries.

Glimmers of wishes that dance afar,
Guided by the light of a distant star.
A tapestry of night, woven tight,
Stitching dreams into the heart of night.

Luminous Secrets of the Timeless Grove

In the heart of woods where shadows play,
Whispers of time linger, drift away.
Ancient oaks stand tall and wise,
Guardians of secrets beneath the skies.

Moss carpets the ground like emerald sheets,
Where forest magic softly beats.
Every rustle tells a vibrant tale,
Of light that shines when the daylight pales.

In twilight glow, the fireflies dance,
A shimmering waltz, a fleeting chance.
Unveiling dreams in luminescent hue,
A symphony of night, old yet new.

Beneath the branches, magic weaves,
Threads of starlight, life it breathes.
Each moment captured, forever stays,
In the grove's embrace, time softly sways.

Mysteries stir in the humid air,
Voices of nature, a sacred prayer.
In every sigh, the world finds peace,
As light uncovers what shadows cease.

Murmurs Carried by the Moonlit Breeze

Underneath the cloak of night's embrace,
Breezes whisper softly, secrets trace.
The world sleeps beneath a silver shawl,
Hushed are the echoes, quiet the call.

Moonbeams sprinkle light on tender skin,
Inviting dreams to stir within.
Every gust, a gentle lover's sigh,
Carrying stories from the sky.

Fluttering leaves dance to their tune,
In perfect harmony with the moon.
Nature's chorus, a sweet refrain,
A lullaby that soothes all pain.

Starry whispers guide the nightingale,
A serenade that will never pale.
With every note, hearts intertwine,
Cradled in the night, so divine.

The cool breeze wraps around like a shawl,
Filling the air with love's sweet call.
In these moments, lost in the dream,
Life flows gently like the softest stream.

Echoing Spellcraft Beneath the Starry Veil

In the cloak of night where shadows dwell,
Magic awakens, casting its spell.
Under the stars, forgotten lands,
Whispers of wonder slip through our hands.

Ancient runes in the soft light show,
Stories of souls that long ago glow.
Entranced by the beauty of tales untold,
The universe fills with wonders bold.

Spellbound by the dance of the cosmic fire,
Every heartbeat resonates with desire.
As dreams awaken on this sacred ground,
Echoes of magic start to resound.

Beneath the veil of a star-strewn night,
Fates intertwine in shimmering light.
A tapestry woven with care and grace,
In the heart of darkness, a warm embrace.

In every spark that lights the sky,
Lies the promise of what may lie.
A spell of beauty, boundless and free,
Forever echoing in you and me.

Secrets Beneath the Celestial Canopy

Whispers dance in the night sky,
As stars spill tales from above.
Hidden dreams in shadows lie,
Wrapped in the warmth of love.

Beneath the vastness, secrets blend,
In every flicker, stories weave.
A cradle where the heavens bend,
Awakening hope for those who believe.

Shimmering lights in cosmic flight,
Scribe the paths of the divine.
Echoes of time in silence bright,
Map the journeys we call mine.

With every glance, a whispered sigh,
The universe beckons near.
In midnight's arms, we dare to fly,
Chasing shadows, casting fear.

So gather 'round, under moons that glow,
And share the tales of endless night.
Together we'll unlock the flow,
Of stars and dreams, in pure delight.

Light Through the Veil of Magic

A tapestry of dreams unfolds,
With threads of silver, gold, and hue.
Secrets whispered, legends told,
In a world where wishes come true.

Through the veil, a flicker bright,
Sparks a journey, wild and free.
In shadows deep, we find the light,
Guiding steps to mystery.

Winds carry scents of ancient tales,
Through forests dense, where wonders wake.
The heart of night, where magic hails,
Awakens paths we dare to take.

With laughter shared and hearts aligned,
We dance beneath the glowing moons.
In every glance, enchantment finds,
The rhythm of our ancient tunes.

So let us walk where dreams ignite,
And fate entwines the bold and brave.
In realms where shadows kiss the light,
We'll chase the magic that we crave.

Resonance of the Starlit Glade

In a glade where night unfolds,
Whispers echo through the trees.
The starlit sky, a tale retold,
Breathes life into the evening breeze.

Dancing shadows play their part,
While luminescence gently glows.
Nature sings, a beating heart,
In harmony that ebbs and flows.

With each step, a story stirs,
In rustling leaves, in creatures' flight.
The magic of the night concurs,
Transforming darkness into light.

Crickets serenade the night,
Their song, a chorus soft and clear.
Through the glade, a sense of right,
Wraps around us, drawing near.

In this sacred space we find,
The pulse of worlds both old and new.
A resonance that binds mankind,
With nature's call, we start anew.

Ghostly Glimmers in Twilight

When twilight casts its soft embrace,
The world transforms to ethereal glow.
Ghostly figures drift in grace,
Among the whispers that softly flow.

In the fading light, secrets roam,
Through shadows deep and dreams long past.
Every flicker feels like home,
In the realm where moments last.

Echoes linger, stories untold,
Each sigh a bridge to paths once crossed.
In twilight's grasp, we gently hold,
The memories cherished, never lost.

As stars emerge in the dusk's caress,
The night unfolds its tender grace.
In darkness, we too, are blessed,
Guided by the light we trace.

So let us wander through this haze,
Where ghostly glimmers softly play.
In twilight's charm, we lose our gaze,
And find the magic night conveys.

Mirror of the Enchanted Veil

In whispers soft, the shadows play,
A surface gleams, showing the sway.
Reflected dreams in twilight shine,
A hidden world where stars align.

Through silver strands, the secrets glide,
The heart unveils what souls confide.
In silent depths, truths intertwine,
Each glimmer tells of fate's design.

A gentle touch on misty air,
A call to rise, a chance to dare.
In every glance, a story told,
Of ancient paths and hearts of gold.

The mirror whispers, beckons near,
With gleaming hope, dispelling fear.
Within its depths, horizons blend,
A timeless bond that will not end.

In twilight's arms, we lose our way,
To find the magic in the fray.
Through enchanted veils, we sail so bold,
In reflections bright, our dreams unfold.

Through the Twilight Canopy

Beneath the leaves, the shadows dance,
Whispers of night in a fleeting glance.
The stars above begin to peek,
In quiet woods, the shadows speak.

Through branches thick, a silver light,
Guides our way through creeping night.
The air is thick with tales untold,
As moonlit paths begin to unfold.

With every step, the magic swells,
As hidden secrets weave their spells.
In twilight's grasp, all dreams ignite,
Beneath the cloak of velvet night.

A symphony of silence calls,
Encircles us within its thralls.
We walk the line of dusk and dawn,
Through the canopy, we are reborn.

In every rustle, stories rise,
With echoes rich beneath the skies.
Through twilight's gate, we find our place,
In nature's arms, we slow our pace.

Flickering Tales of the Astral Realm

In twilight's glow, the stars conspire,
To weave a world of dreams and fire.
Flickers bright, a cosmic dance,
Celestial tales in chance's trance.

Whispers carry through the night,
Glimmers of truth in endless flight.
Galaxies spin, in silence twirl,
Each fragment speaks, a mystery unfurl.

Through vast expanses, shadows roam,
In galaxies far, we find a home.
From stardust born, our spirits soar,
To realms unknown, forevermore.

In astral dreams, we find our way,
Where light and dark in harmony play.
A flickering brush on canvas wide,
Tales of the cosmos, deep inside.

So close your eyes and drift away,
Embrace the night where wonders lay.
For in the heart of the astral scene,
Lies flickering tales, where we have been.

The Dance of Forgotten Flames

In the silence of the moon's bright glow,
Forgotten flames begin to flow.
In shadows deep, their embers sway,
A dance of light, in disarray.

Once fierce and bright, now whispers soft,
In swirling echoes, memories loft.
Each flicker tells of passion's past,
A story woven, shadows cast.

The night unfolds with every turn,
While silent hearts in silence yearn.
For bonds that flicker, hearts that know,
In every flame, our spirits grow.

As they twirl free in the softest air,
The dance ignites a truth laid bare.
In every movement, a life reclaimed,
In forgotten flames, we are named.

So let us gather 'neath the stars,
Embrace the spark, erase our scars.
For in this dance of flames so bright,
We find our way through endless night.

www.ingramcontent.com/pod-product-compliance
Ingram Content Group UK Ltd.
Pitfield, Milton Keynes, MK11 3LW, UK
UKHW021634200125
4187UKWH00003B/130